football's new wave

Kurt Warner

Can't Keep Him Down

BY

MARK STEWART

THE MILLBROOK PRESS
BROOKFIELD, CONNECTICUT

M

THE MILLBROOK PRESS

Produced by
BITTERSWEET PUBLISHING
John Sammis, President
and
TEAM STEWART, INC.
RESEARCHED AND EDITED BY MIKE KENNEDY

Series Design and Electronic Page Makeup by
JAFFE ENTERPRISES
Ron Jaffe

Printed in the United States of America

Published by
The Millbrook Press, Inc.
2 Old New Milford Road
Brookfield, Connecticut   06804

www.millbrookpress.com

Library of Congress Cataloging-in-Publication Data

Stewart, Mark.
    Kurt Warner: can't keep him down / by Mark Stewart
    p.   cm.   — (Football's new wave)
    Includes index.
    ISBN 0-7613-1953-0 (lib. bdg.)
    1. Warner, Kurt, 1971–   —Juvenile literature. 2. Football players—United States—Biography—
Juvenile literature. [1. Warner, Kurt, 1971– . 2. Football players.] I. Title: Can't keep him down. II.
Title. III. Series
GV939.W36 S84 2001
796.332'092--dc21
[B]   00-040213

1 3 5 7 9 10 8 6 4 2

Contents

Destiny's Child

chapter 1

"I've always had confidence, and I've always believed that I could be successful."

— KURT WARNER

What is the difference between a superstar athlete and an "ordinary" pro? When it comes to physical talent, not very much. Some call the thing that separates the good player from the great one *heart*. Others call it *drive*. It is the ability to reach down again and again—often when things look their gloomiest—and find that little extra something to help you succeed. Whatever it is, wherever it comes from, it is a rare and wonderful thing. The players who have it are the ones we love most. Kurt Warner has that special something. And long before it got him to the Super Bowl, it got him through some very rough times.

Kurt was born on June 22, 1971, in Burlington, Iowa. When he thinks back to his early childhood, he does not remember much happiness. His parents, Gene and Sue, did not get along very well. They were divorced when he was four. Although they tried to explain to Kurt and his older brother, Matt, why it was best for everyone to end the marriage, the boys were too young to understand.

No one who knew Kurt as a kid ever dreamed he would be a pro football star. Except Kurt, of course.

Regis High School was renamed Xavier High School after Kurt graduated in 1989. But football is still king on campus.

Kurt took the divorce badly. Sometimes, to "punish" his mom, he would hold his breath until he passed out. Kurt and Matt became very close during this time. Although they still had contact with their father, they knew that when it came down to it, they had to rely on each other and trust each other. This bond grew even stronger after Sue remarried in 1981. The boys' stepfather did not like them and often ordered them down to the basement so they would not be in his way. Kurt and Matt also noticed that their mother had a lot of cuts and bruises—he was beating her up.

Realizing her mistake, Sue ended this marriage quickly. She decided it might be best if she and her sons tried to go it alone for a while. This meant everyone had extra responsibilities. Kurt and Matt had to do all of the chores around the house and had to keep themselves occupied (and out of trouble) while their mother worked three jobs to keep enough money coming into the house.

To fill the hours when his mother was not around, Kurt decided to get more involved in sports. Kurt's first "team" experience was in flag football at the Jane Boyd Community

Kurt would have enjoyed owning this card back in the early 1980s, when he dreamed of being a Dallas Cowboys receiver, like Drew Pearson.

Center. He was a terrific player. He was a fast, smart runner who could instantly make sense of the swirl of bodies in front of him. Often, Kurt would run through a swarm of defenders and emerge on the other side with his flags still flapping. "In flag football, we played against the local YMCA teams and never lost a game in the three or four years I played," Kurt claims. "I was very good—I was fast then."

Kurt soon moved into tackle football. Before his first practice, he told his mother that he thought he would make the pros some day. He wanted to be a wide receiver for the Dallas Cowboys. That dream got sidetracked, however, when he was told he weighed too much to play receiver. Unfortunately, the size restrictions for seventh and eight graders limited him to the line. This upset Kurt. What sense did it make for him to play a position where he never touched the ball? He knew what his talent was: He had a "nose" for the end zone. Kurt hated playing offensive tackle so much he even thought about quitting football. Playing the drums in the marching band seemed like it would be more fun than playing the line. "It was boring," he says.

Did You Know?

To give Kurt the confidence to trust his blockers and stand in the pocket, Regis High coach Jim Padlock invented a game called "Kill Kurt." Kurt had to take the snap, find his pass protection, then stay in the pocket—without passing!—until a defensive player finally barreled in and creamed him. Looking back, however, he realizes how important this drill was. "It's something that now is probably my strongest suit," Kurt says proudly. "Guys can be in my face and it doesn't faze me!"

During the summer of 1985, a lot of Kurt's "baby fat" was replaced by lean muscle. When he showed up for freshman tryouts at Regis High School, the coaches told the boys to line up so they could get a look at them. Kurt stood out immediately—he was much bigger than the other boys. Then the coaches asked everyone to throw the ball as far as they could. Kurt threw it farther than anyone. What coach Jim Padlock did not tell his players was that he had no idea who would play quarterback that season. They were *all* trying out!

"I've had some hard times, but everyone's had some hard times. All those things have done is strengthen my character and strengthen me as a person, as well as a player."

KURT WARNER

Well, guess who Coach Padlock picked?

At first, Kurt was reluctant. "I didn't want to switch at all," he laughs. "I wanted to be a receiver. I wanted to play tight end!"

Kurt kept insisting he would make a perfect tight end. He could see an opponent's soft spots and tell where the open areas would be just by glancing down the field from his position at the line of scrimmage. Padlock said the team would like Kurt to use this skill as a passer. Plus, he had proved he had the toughness and endurance to play quarterback during his years as a lineman. Finally, Kurt agreed to give it a try. And as everyone predicted, quarterbacking came very naturally to Kurt. "Once I started playing the position, it was obviously so much more fun, because I got the ball every play and got to make all the decisions," he says.

By the end of his freshman season Kurt was the team's leader. He also developed the confidence to try other sports. Soon he was a star on the Regis High basketball and baseball teams. By his senior year, Kurt was among the top all-around athletes in Iowa. He made the All-State football team and got to play in the North-South Shrine Bowl, a charity All-Star game that draws college scouts from around the country. Kurt led the North squad to a thrilling, last-second victory.

At the traditional pregame dinner, a guest speaker looked into the faces of the 100 or so high-school seniors and tried to put football into perspective for them. Most of the boys were good enough to earn a scholarship to college. He urged each player to take advantage of this gift and make the most of his education. Even though they all dreamed of going on to play in the National Football League, maybe two percent would ever get a chance, he said. A friend named Stacey Martens was at Kurt's table that night. He asked Kurt what he planned to do after football.

"I'll be in that two percent," he replied.

Stuck on the Bench

chapter 1

> *"Mom, I'm quitting.*
> *I'm coming home."*
> — KURT WARNER

Kurt Warner may have been a "big fish" in Iowa, but Iowa is a "small pond" in the world of college football recruiting. A lot of colleges believed that, although Kurt was a superb high-school quarterback, he had reached the "ceiling" of his talents. In other words, there was nothing the scouts saw that suggested he would get much better. In fact, not a single major college made him a scholarship offer. "I was probably the best quarterback in the state of Iowa," he says. "I would have thought that at least the University of Iowa or Iowa State would have contacted me."

Kurt did receive attention from a handful of smaller schools. The University of Northern Iowa (UNI), located in nearby Cedar Falls, offered him a partial scholarship to play for its team. He would have to sit out his first year as a "red shirt," then earn a place as a backup quarterback. If it worked out, the school would convert him to a full scholarship and pay all of his expenses. You have to start somewhere, Kurt figured, so it might as well be close to home. He accepted the offer and enrolled in 1989.

UNI head coach Terry Allen

The coach of the UNI Panthers was Terry Allen. Allen told Kurt to be prepared to sit on the bench for a couple of years before he got a shot at the starting job. During that time, he would have to polish his skills and learn the team's offense. UNI had one of the best Division I-AA teams in the nation, and Kurt was not ready to step in and take over.

Kurt agreed, and did as coach Allen asked. Deep down, though, he believed he would get a chance much sooner. After all, isn't that how the story always goes? Doesn't the star always have to beat the odds and win the job when no one gives him a chance?

Kurt would indeed beat the odds, but it would not happen the way he anticipated. After his red-shirt season, he sat on the Panthers' bench for three more seasons. UNI's quarterback was Jay Johnson. He was a year ahead of Kurt. Johnson had put up amazing numbers as a sophomore in 1990. By 1992 he had worked with the team's other offensive stars—Tank Corner, Kenny Shedd, and Chris Nuss—for a couple of seasons, so Coach Allen saw no reason to mess with success and give Kurt a start. The team reached the Division I-AA championship game, but Kurt barely played at all that year. "That was the hardest stint I've ever been through," he says, "just sitting on the bench, knowing I wasn't going to play."

Kurt realized just how unimportant he was in Allen's eyes after the team's very first game in 1992, against McNeese State. The coach had promised Kurt he would get some snaps, but the game went right down to the wire and Kurt never set foot on the field. Even though UNI won, 21–18, Kurt was furious afterward. He called his mother. Then he called his father. He told them both that he saw no reason to keep playing football. His parents each told him to stick it out, get his degree, and wait for his chance.

When Kurt finally got a chance to start for Northern Iowa in 1993,
he became the Gateway Conference's top quarterback.

The following summer, Kurt began to see the big picture. Allen had played Johnson for three seasons because he was a good, experienced quarterback. It was nothing personal. With Johnson graduated, now Kurt was "the man."

He soon discovered that being "the man" was a lot harder than he thought it would be. In the season's first two games, Northern Iowa lost, 27–10, to McNeese State and, 45–42, to Wyoming. In the Wyoming game, Kurt separated his shoulder and had to sit out the second half. All he could do was think about the four years he had waited for this chance, and now it might be slipping away. Well, there was no way he was going to let that happen. He suited up for the next game, the home opener against Jacksonville State, and did not tell the coaches how badly his shoulder hurt. "I proba-

Coaches have always loved Kurt's ability to take a hit and still throw a tight spiral.

bly shouldn't have played," he admits now. "I couldn't throw very well. But I was going to do whatever I could to get on the field. I wasn't going to miss it."

Despite the worst passing performance of Kurt's life, the Panthers won. The defense came through and paved the way to an easy 35–14 victory. Southwest Texas State was next, and Kurt (now fitted with a special protective pad) had an excellent game in a 34–13 win. Kurt made it three in a row with a tough 20–14 triumph over Southwest Missouri State. The Panthers won twice more, then lost a squeaker to Western Illinois. With the conference championship on the line, Kurt came through again, finishing the year with three straight wins—including a 49–17 blowout of Southern Illinois.

Kurt's final numbers were pretty good for a first-year quarterback. He finished with 2,747 passing yards and 17 touchdowns, and led the Panthers into the Division I-AA playoffs. Sometimes he had been brilliant, sometimes ordinary. But never was Kurt overwhelmed by anything that happened in a game. And no matter how hard he got hit, or how badly the breaks went against him, he got up and came right back at the other team.

When the season was over, Kurt was proud of what he had done. He was also very excited about the future. In his mind, he had taken a major step toward his dream—he felt he was ready to hook up with an NFL team.

The woman with whom Kurt hoped to share this dream had also entered his life. One night during his senior year, Kurt went with some friends to a country-music club. He was not much of a party animal, and quickly became bored. As he scanned the crowd, he noticed a woman taking line-dancing lessons. There seemed to be something special about her. Kurt worked up the courage to start talking to her, and soon they were exchanging the stories of their lives.

Brenda Meoni was an ex-Marine and a single mother of two young children. Her son, Zach, had been dropped on his head as an infant and suffered brain damage. The tragic accident had so devastated the family that it led to divorce. Now she was on her own, coping with a situation that most people would not wish on their worst enemy.

> ## Did You Know?
> Kurt was named to the All-Gateway Conference squad, and was the conference's Offensive Player of the Year.

Usually, when Brenda told men about her life, they found some convenient way to disappear. She was bright, beautiful, and very engaging, but she had yet to meet someone willing to share her complicated life. To her surprise, Kurt was fascinated. The next day, he knocked on her door and asked if he could meet her kids. He soon fell in love with the entire family. "She was a strong woman, like my mother," Kurt says of Brenda. "I think that's why I fell for her. My friends said, 'You're crazy—enjoy the single life.' But that's not me."

college stats

Season	Team	Attempts	Completions	Yards	Touchdowns
1990	Northern Iowa	13	8	141	2
1991	Northern Iowa	25	15	23	0
1992	Northern Iowa	18	5	69	0
1993	Northern Iowa	296	173	2,747	17
Totals		**352**	**201**	**2,980**	**19**

career highlights

Gateway Conference Player of the Year 1993

Big Man on a Little Field

chapter

*"I was making $5.50 an hour...
and I was darn happy to get it!"*

— KURT WARNER

For college players hoping to join the NFL, the first months of the year are critical. That is when the teams hold their scouting combines, where more than 300 potential pros are timed, tested, and measured in every conceivable way. Every professional team sends its top talent scouts to the combines, where a good performance can make a player, and a bad performance can break one.

Of course, you have to be invited to the combines before anyone takes you seriously. And when no invitations came for Kurt, he realized that he had thought a lot more of his senior season than the pros had. When draft day came and went without Kurt's phone ringing, it dealt a second major blow to his dream of playing in the NFL. "They just skipped over me," he says. "Nobody knew who I was."

Luckily, a couple of teams had watched him at UNI, and they contacted him after the draft. Although a typical NFL team carries just three quarterbacks, often more than a half-dozen are invited to try out. They provide extra arms and extra bodies for all of the extra players in camp, and every so often a young passer catches a coach's eye. When Kurt was invited to camp by the Green Bay Packers, he grabbed the opportunity.

Kurt played pretty well, but did not make the team. While he was in camp, however, he got an idea of what it would take to make an NFL roster. The quarterbacks who did make the Packers, Mark Brunell

Brenda cheers Kurt from the stands. She helped him stay focused during some difficult years.

and Ty Detmer, knew a lot more about the details of the pro game. They had come from better college programs and had been around long enough to develop a feel for what the position called for. "I would have liked a better chance at it," Kurt says of the Green Bay backup job, "but I also knew that I wasn't strong enough, or near ready."

After he was cut, Kurt returned from camp and moved in with Brenda's family in Waterloo, Iowa. She and her kids were living with her parents, and they welcomed Kurt

Kurt had to speed up his game to succeed in Arena Football.

as one of their own. To help make ends meet in the crowded house, Kurt needed to find a job. He went to a local supermarket, asked to talk to the manager, and before he knew it he was stocking shelves at the Hy-Vee. It was not a great job, and it did not pay very well. But Kurt was just happy that he and Brenda were together.

As often happens in life, when one door closed for Kurt another one opened. He received a call from John Gregory, the newly hired coach of the Iowa Barnstormers. The Barnstormers were a member of Arena League Football, which holds its season during the spring and summer. Arena Football is played indoors, on a field that is roughly the size of a hockey rink. There are only eight players per side, and the action is fast and furious. Gregory wanted Kurt to quarterback his team in 1995.

Back then, most football fans thought Arena Football was a joke. Kurt had seen a few games on TV and thought it looked terrible, too. However, he did recognize many of the names on the jerseys—a lot of the guys had been really good college players. Still, when Gregory first talked to him, Kurt was not sure he wanted to get involved. Finally, he saw the opportunity for what it was: a chance to play pro ball and improve his skills. Kurt accepted. It sure beat working in the supermarket!

As Kurt prepared for his first season of Arena Football, he made the mistake many college stars do. He thought it was just a smaller, easier version of football. He did not

With his strong, accurate arm, Kurt could throw touchdowns from any spot on the tiny Arena League fields.

realize that the less room you have to work with, the harder it is to move your team forward. In his first game—an exhibition against the St. Louis Stampede—he was humiliated. Everything was going too fast for him. Receivers were open, then they were not. Defenders were one place, then another, then in his face. Kurt was making his decisions a half-beat slower than everyone else on the field, and the Barnstormers got creamed.

Between Arena Football seasons, Kurt continued to hope for a shot at the NFL. But no tryout invitations came in 1995 or 1996. Kurt was beginning to wonder if he would ever get another chance. He would talk about

Did You Know?

Jim Foster, owner of the Iowa Barnstormers, called Kurt "Houdini" for his ability to escape from the most impossible situations and win games.

these fears with Brenda, and she would try to keep his spirits up. She knew he was a fierce competitor, so the best way to keep him focused was to tell him that, for now, he had to concentrate on being the best Arena Football player he could be.

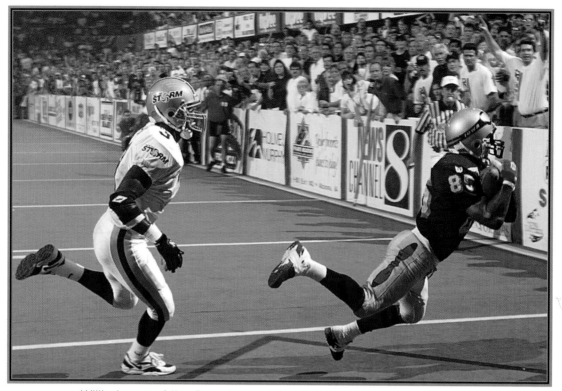

*Willis Jacox of the Barnstormers hauls in a perfect pass from Kurt
for a touchdown during the 1996 Arena Bowl.*

In April 1996, as Kurt was beginning his second Arena Football season, he received
some terrible news. Brenda called him to say that her parents had been killed. A torna-
do had ripped through their neighborhood and swept their house away. Kurt was devastated. For the next several weeks he was in a state of shock, as he and Brenda and the
kids tried to cope with this senseless tragedy.

When the season started, Kurt just could not get it together. He played poorly in
the first four games. Finally, in the fifth game, Coach Gregory had to pull him out.
Kurt's father, watching on television at home, turned off the set. It was the first time
Gene Warner had ever seen his son give up, and he could not bear to watch anymore.

As it turned out, Gene missed the most important moment in Kurt's football life.
Something came over him on the Barnstormer bench that night. As Kurt watched his
teammates struggle to pull themselves out of the hole he had dug for them, everything
became crystal clear. They say you have to hit rock bottom before you can start working your way to the top, and maybe that is what happened.

With Iowa down by five points and time running out, Gregory turned to his bench and saw the new fire in Kurt's eye. He told him to put on his helmet and get back in the game. Six plays later, Kurt got the Barnstormers into the end zone. That day, a legend was born.

Kurt Warner became Arena Football's best quarterback in 1996. He was even better in 1997. Both years, he led the Barnstormers to the Arena Bowl championship game. In 1997 he threw a mind-boggling 79 touchdown passes. It was not just that Kurt was putting up huge numbers and winning games. It was that—no matter what obstacle stood before him—he always found a way to overcome it.

Unfortunately, Kurt's reputation for heroics did not reach the NFL. In 1997 and 1998, not one team offered him a job. The job that was offered came from far away: NFL Europe, a developmental league sponsored by the National Football League. NFL Europe has the dual purpose of developing young talent for pro teams in the United States, and at the same time popularizing the game overseas. The team that contacted Kurt was the Admirals, who played in the Dutch city of Amsterdam. Amsterdam's coach, Al Luginbill, had been keeping an eye on Kurt and liked what he saw. He guaranteed Kurt that he would be the starting quarterback if he accepted the offer to play in Europe.

Kurt told Luginbill that if he was going to leave his wife and children, then he wanted a second guarantee. He said he would play for the Amsterdam Admirals on one condition: that he be "sponsored" by an NFL team. He wanted an NFL club to sign him to a contract that would automatically bring him into the league if he did well in Europe. Luginbill said that he understood, and that he would do his best to accommodate Kurt.

Did You Know?

Kurt and Brenda were married in the fall of 1997. A few days before the wedding, the Chicago Bears asked Kurt to work out for them. He told them his honeymoon came first!

arena league *stats*

SEASON	TEAM	ATTEMPTS	COMPLETIONS	YARDS	TOUCHDOWNS
1995	Barnstormers	400	239	2,980	43
1996	Barnstormers	422	259	3,336	61
1997	Barnstormers	498	322	4,149	79
TOTALS		**1,320**	**820**	**10,465**	**183**

career *highlights*

Arena League MVP . . . . 1996 & 1997

The football world is like a giant spider web. Everyone is connected to everyone else. Between high school, college, and the pros, there are so many coaches and players that have worked together that rarely is someone more than a couple of phone calls away from an old friend. This can kill a player trying to shed a bad reputation. But it can also work wonders for a good guy like Kurt.

Mike Kolling recommended Kurt to the St. Louis Rams.

Luginbill phoned Charley Armey, head of player personnel for the St. Louis Rams. Many years earlier, Armey had coached high-school ball in Minnesota. His prize pupil back then had been quarterback Mike Kolling, who was later on the coaching staff for Northern Iowa when Kurt played there. Armey contacted Kolling and asked him for his opinion on Kurt. Kolling told him that they had worked together well, and that he thought Armey should take a chance and sign him. Kurt came to an agreement with the Rams in December of 1997, then headed for Amsterdam to begin the 1998 season.

Dutch Treat

chapter 4

"Warner's become the patron saint for every free agent beating football's bush leagues."

— MAT EDELSON, SPORTSWRITER

After just a few snaps, Kurt knew the switch from Arena Football back to "regular" football would be easy. And as the NFL Europe season unfolded, he realized the game itself had become easy. Kurt was still playing at the same blinding Arena Football speed—his reads, his footwork, his decision-making, and his release were quicker than anyone else's. With more blockers, more runners, more receivers, and a more spread-out defense, everything else seemed to be moving in slow motion. Imagine how easy football would be if you could move at full speed while everyone else was going in slo-mo. Well, that is how Kurt felt during his year with the Amsterdam Admirals.

"It really was my way to open some eyes," Kurt says of his decision to play overseas, "that I could compete on a big field and do all the things that I wasn't called upon to do in the Arena League. It just gave me a chance to reorient myself."

The statistics show that it was everyone else who was doing the re-orienting. Kurt led NFL Europe with 2,101 yards, 165 completions, and 15 touchdowns. The

NFL Europe *stats*

SEASON	TEAM	ATTEMPTS	COMPLETIONS	YARDS	TOUCHDOWNS
1998	Admirals	326	165	2,101	15

Admirals were league champions, and Kurt's contract was picked up by the Rams, who were already in training camp for the 1998 season. "It gave me the confidence to know I could come into the NFL and succeed," Kurt says of his super summer with the Admirals.

After devouring the St. Louis playbook and getting a feel for the various personalities on the team, Kurt slid easily into the role promised him: third-string quarterback.

The Rams' starter in 1998 was Tony Banks, an amazing athlete who had also played professional baseball. The backup was 36-year-old Steve Bono, a former Pro Bowl quarterback. The Rams had some good players on offense, including receiver Isaac Bruce, who once caught more than 100 passes in a season. The defense was not bad, either. There was a good mix of young players and veterans.

What Kurt liked most about the Rams was how hard the players played for their coach, Dick Vermeil. A greatly admired young coach back in the 1970s, Vermeil had returned to the sidelines after a 14-year retirement. He was tough and emotional, but the players knew he would stick by them if they gave everything they had.

Dick Vermeil demanded the best from his players, and gave them his best in return.

Trent Green was slated to be the St. Louis starter in 1999, but a preseason knee injury kept him out of action.

Kurt spent almost the entire 1998 season watching from the bench. He felt bad for Banks when St. Louis' two main offensive weapons, Bruce and running back Greg Hill, went down with injuries. The fans booed the Rams all year. They booed Banks for not single-handedly pulling the team through. They booed Vermeil, and claimed he was now too old and out-of-touch to coach. The booing grew louder and louder as the Rams lost nine of their final 11 games. In the season finale, against the San Francisco 49ers, Kurt finally got a chance to play. He completed four passes for 39 yards.

After the season, the Rams released Bono and began shopping Banks around in a trade. That meant Kurt would go into 1999 as the Rams' number-two quarterback. The only question was, who would be number one?

The answer was free agent Trent Green. In 1998 he had come off the bench to lead the Washington Redskins to victory in six of their last nine games. The Rams also got the backfield star they needed by trading two draft picks to the Indianapolis Colts for Pro Bowl runner Marshall Faulk. Faulk was available

Did You Know?

The Rams are actually the fourth NFL team to call St. Louis home. In the early days of the NFL, St. Louis hosted the All-Stars (1923) and the Gunners (1934). Neither team lasted more than a few games. In 1960 the Cardinals moved from Chicago to St. Louis and stayed there for 28 seasons. Their first win came against—who else?— the (Los Angeles) Rams!

The addition of multitalented Marshall Faulk made the 1999 Rams one of football's most dangerous offensive teams.

because the Colts planned to take Edgerrin James in the college draft, and did not want two stars fighting over the ball in their backfield. Vermeil could not have been happier about his offense. With Green, he had a reliable signal-caller who could get the ball to his receivers. With Faulk, he had someone who could score on a run or a pass—and keep defenses from keying on the Rams' receivers.

The receivers were an exciting group. Besides Bruce, there were veteran Ricky Proehl and first-round draft pick Torry Holt, an All-American from North Carolina State. Also in the mix was Az-Zahir Hakim, a fleet-footed pass-catcher who knew how to get open. The offensive line, much improved with the addition of free agent Adam Timmerman and the development of young stars Fred Miller and Orlando Pace, would give Green all the time he needed to put the ball in his receiver's hands.

In August the Rams learned that football can be a cruel game. During the team's third exhibition contest, Green took a brutal hit from behind and blew out his knee. He was gone for the year. Up to that moment, it looked as if Green would be the NFL's

"Cinderella" story in 1999. A local boy from Vianney High School in suburban St. Louis, he had come home and done a great job. Prior to his injury, in fact, Green had been practically perfect. Only four of his passes that entire summer had fallen incomplete. After the game, the emotional Vermeil was in tears. Everything had gone so well, all of his planning had paid off—and now the season was lost.

After the shock of losing Green wore off, Vermeil and his staff looked around and decided they still might be able to contend. The Rams had been doing well not just because of Green. Everyone was playing well around him. In fact, their new first-string quarterback, Kurt Warner, had been having a great summer, too.

In the final preseason contest, against the Detroit Lions, Kurt got plenty of snaps. He looked nervous at times, but when the team needed him to make a big play, he found a way to do it. He also made several throws that Green would not have been strong enough to try. By the end of the game, Kurt was in command of the offense. He had won the respect of his teammates, and had the coaches smiling behind their clipboards on the sidelines. Maybe, just maybe, Kurt could get the job done.

The Warner File

KURT'S FAVORITE...

Number . . . . 13.
He wears it to prove there's no such thing as bad luck.

Non-Football Job . . . . Sportscasting.
He has a degree in Communications

Flower . . . . Rose

Breakfast Cereal . . . . Warner's Crunch Time

"I think there are still people out there who aren't quite sure if I'm for real. It is a strange story."

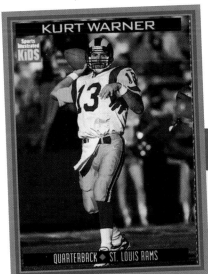

KURT WARNER

13

QUARTERBACK ◆ ST. LOUIS RAMS

Did You Know?

At the start of 1999, Kurt Warner trading cards were worth a few pennies. A few weeks later they were the hottest cards in the hobby.

*Even though he knew deep down that he could succeed in the NFL,
Kurt is still amazed at his incredible rise to fame.*

Chance of a Lifetime

chapter

"I've always known that if I got the right opportunity and the right system, I could be successful."

— KURT WARNER

I n Kurt's mind, there was no question that he was capable of being a productive NFL quarterback. On the day that Green was injured, and panic filled the clubhouse, Kurt sat calmly in front of his locker. He knew this was the chance he had dreamed about since he was a little kid, and after all the years and all the miles and all the waiting and wondering, there was no way he was going to to do anything but succeed. Kurt also knew that he would be a subject of great concern and curiosity. "An unknown guy has the

The sight of Trent Green hobbling through the clubhouse scared many of the Rams. But Kurt was absolutely certain that he could get the job done.

> *"We had an opportunity in the off-season to get another quarterback. If we hadn't felt great about Kurt, we would have done something then."*
>
> MIKE MARTZ

spotlight thrust upon him, and everybody wants to know the same things," he says. "Who is he? What's he about? And can he get the job done?"

Of course, Kurt realized that no one would care about the answers if he messed up. One bad game and the fans would be howling to have "Mr. Unknown" replaced. He did not take this personally, however. Kurt knew that Dick Vermeil and offensive coordinator Mike Martz had faith in his ability. He just wanted to reward their faith in him as quickly as possible.

Kurt did just that in the season's first game. With the home crowd cheering wildly, he led the Rams to an easy 27–10 win over the Baltimore Ravens. Kurt connected on 28 of 44 passes for 309 yards and three touchdowns. He also stayed in the pocket and took vicious hits in order to complete important passes. The Ravens were not one of the NFL's top teams, but Kurt could not have played any better.

Kurt's first big test came against the Atlanta Falcons in the season's second game. The Falcons had gone to the Super Bowl the season before and were favorites to win the division again, ahead of the 49ers and the Rams. But on this day, the Rams looked like division winners.

Did You Know?

Kurt's receivers soon began calling themselves the "Warner Brothers."

Kurt gave the NFC champs a taste of Arena Football, as he sent receivers darting in and around the Atlanta defense and hit them with quick passes before the Falcons could react. He finished with three more touchdowns, and the Rams had their second-straight decisive victory.

Kurt holds his ground against linebacker Ray Lewis of the Ravens in the season opener. At 6′ 2″, 225 pounds Kurt is big enough to hang in against the league's most ferocious pass rushers.

The following Sunday, Kurt again threw three touchdown passes, this time against the Cincinnati Bengals. It had been 50 years since a pro had tossed three TDs in his first three starts. The Rams' fourth game, against the hated 49ers, sealed the love affair

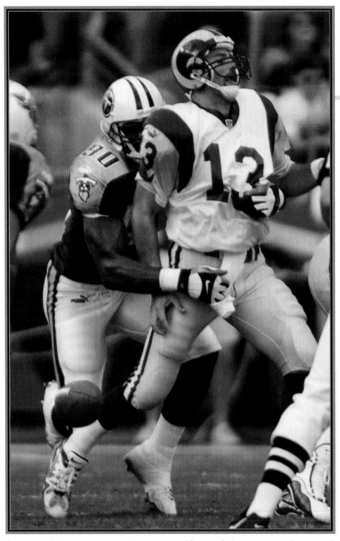

Kurt is stripped of the football by Jevon Kearse of the Titans in the Rams' first loss of the year. These two stars would meet again.

between Kurt and the fans of St. Louis. Normally, Vermeil likes his quarterbacks to look for short passes, then scan farther downfield if no one is open. Everyone in the NFL knew this, including the 49ers. For this meeting, however, Vermeil instructed Kurt to look deep first, then go to the short passes.

This was a great compliment for a veteran coach to pay an inexperienced quarterback. Vermeil was telling Kurt that he not only had a great arm, but that he also had faith in his ability to read defenses quickly enough to pick out a good secondary receiver. Kurt knew this was a major vote of confidence, and was determined to prove to the team he deserved it. In the first quarter, he tore the San Francisco defense to shreds. He threw for 177 yards and led the team to three scores. The game was over at the half, and the Rams coasted to a 42–20 win.

Warner-mania had officially begun. Every magazine wanted to interview Kurt. Every newspaper reporter wanted to know everything about him. Millions of fans surfed the Internet to pick up information on him. And all that anyone around the league could talk about was this guy from nowhere who was eating up the NFL.

The 49ers did not have any answers, but they could tell you one thing: Wherever this guy came from, he was no rookie. He had all the moves of a veteran. He did the little things the fans never see. On his first touchdown against San Francisco, for instance, he pump-faked the entire secondary out of their shorts. And every time they thought they had figured Kurt out, he showed them something that they never expected.

Early in the season, the St. Louis coaches tried to simplify the offense for Kurt so that he would not be overwhelmed. By mid-season, Mike Martz was giving him more and more plays every week. Whatever he threw at Kurt, Kurt threw at his opponents. And whatever he threw at opponents seemed to work.

Everything else was going well for the Rams, too. In particular, the defense had come together beautifully. Cat-quick linemen Kevin Carter and D'Marco Farr created havoc in the trenches, young Grant Wistrom played like a bull in a china shop, and veteran Sam Agnew was there to pick up the pieces and make big stops on key downs. The line-backers, led by Todd Collins and Mike Jones, played beautifully behind this line; the pass defenders, led by Keith Lyle and Todd Lyght, stopped most everything that came their way. The defense's lone weakness—its inability to stop a power running game—was helped by the fact that bruising runners Jamal Anderson of the Falcons and Ricky Williams of the New Orleans Saints were injured most of the year. That turned four possible losses into four easy victories. With injuries and age overcoming the 49ers, the Rams had a clear shot at the division title—their first since 1985.

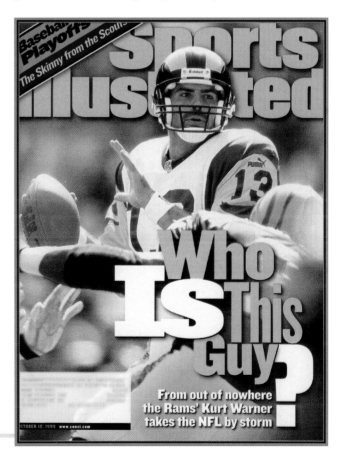

This October 18 SPORTS ILLUSTRATED *cover says it all.*

Kurt got them there with a flourish, finishing with 41 touchdown passes. Only one other quarterback, the great Dan Marino, had ever thrown more during a season. The Rams won 13 games to set a franchise record, and Kurt was named the league's Player of the Year!

Even in defeat, the Rams looked good. Their toughest game came against the Tennessee Titans, who tried to overwhelm the St. Louis line with blitzes on almost every play. For a while, this strategy worked. But by the second half, Kurt had figured out how to deal with the Titans and began to dissect their defense. He led the team to three touchdowns to make the score 24–21, then drove the Rams down to Tennessee's 20-yard line for the tying field goal attempt. A bad kick by Jeff Wilkens lost the game, but Kurt had sent an important message: "You might be able to stop us for a quarter or two, but give us time and we'll getcha!"

Meet Me In St. Louis

Look at the difference in the stats of these players
before and after they began working with Kurt Warner:

	YEAR	RUNNING YARDS	RECEIVING YARDS	TOUCHDOWNS
MARSHALL FAULK	1998	1,319	908	10
Running Back	1999	1,381	1,048*	12
ISAAC BRUCE	1998	30	457	1
Wide Receiver	1999	32	1,165	12
AZ-ZAHIR HAKIM	1998	30	247	2
Wide Receiver	1999	44	677	8
TORRY HOLT	1998	Played in College		
Wide Receiver	1999	25	788	6
ROBERT HOLCOMBE	1998	230	34	2
Running Back	1999	294	163	5

** FAULK BECAME JUST THE SECOND PLAYER IN NFL HISTORY TO HAVE
1,000 RUNNING AND RECEIVING YARDS IN THE SAME SEASON.*

Road to the Super Bowl

chapter 6

*"I expected to play well,
I expected to lead my team,
and I expected to win."*

— KURT WARNER

Kurt Warner had just completed a season that saw him compile the fifth-highest quarterback rating in history and lead his team to the best record in the conference. In the NFL that earns you a week's rest before your first playoff game, and guarantees you the home-field advantage. Those things help when your goal is winning the Super Bowl, but you still have to make it happen on the field.

The first hurdle for the St. Louis Rams would be the Minnesota Vikings, the winner of the previous week's

By playoff time, Kurt was relaxed and confident.

Kurt spots Isaac Bruce in the clear against the Minnesota Vikings. He hit his star receiver with a perfect touchdown pass.

Wild Card game against the Dallas Cowboys. Kurt knew he could put points on the board against the Minnesota defense, but he also knew the Vikings would score on the Rams. Indeed, at halftime, the Rams trailed by a score of 17–14.

Kurt and the coaches talked about all the different things the Vikings had done, and decided how to combat them in the second half. But to have a chance in the game, the team needed a spark. Normally, it was Kurt who provided the big lift. But in this game he never got the chance. Tony Horne took the opening kickoff in front of his own goal line, cut to his left, and then zipped through a sea of purple and white for a 95-yard touchdown. The Rams were back on top, the Vikings were stunned, and the crowd roared until the stands shook. From there it was easy, as Kurt poured it on and the Rams finished off Minnesota, 49–37.

When reporters asked how it felt to do so well in his first playoff game, Kurt was surprised at the question. He did not think of himself as an inexperienced rookie—didn't they know he had been through the pressure of playoffs and championships in

Kurt acknowledges the cheers of the St. Louis fans as he trots off the field following the Rams' 49-37 victory over the Vikings.

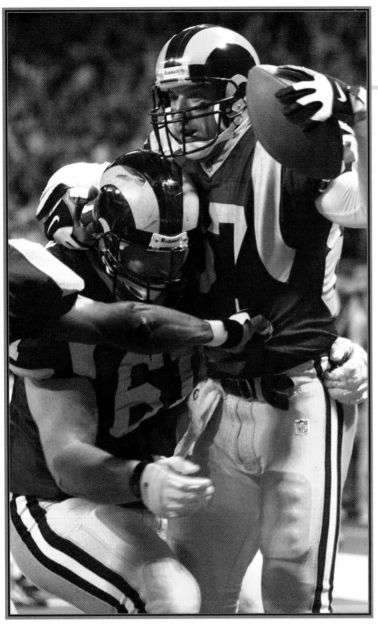

Ricky Proehl is mobbed in the end zone after his great catch against the Tampa Bay Buccaneers.

Arena Football and NFL Europe? "I just think about going out and playing football and winning football games," he explains. "I've done it for a long time, and I didn't expect it to be any different here [in the NFL playoffs]."

The NFC championship game promised to be much less of a scoring duel. The Tampa Bay Buccaneers had a defense known for smothering the run and burying quarterbacks. The Bucs' offense, however, was not very exciting. Mostly, Tampa Bay just pounded opponents into submission with runners Mike Alstott and Warrick Dunn. The team's quarterback, Shaun King, was a rookie with very basic passing skills and no big-game experience. Against this opponent, the Rams countered with a very good defense and one of the greatest offenses in history. The odds said that it would be a low-scoring game, but that the Rams would eventually break through.

Coach Vermeil knew what Tampa Bay coach Tony Dungy was thinking. Dungy hoped his swarming pass rush could force Kurt into a costly interception or fumble. All Tampa Bay needed was a slim lead, and it could eat up the clock and win. Vermeil instructed Kurt to forget about dropping deep into the pocket and looking for long passes. Instead, he was to concentrate on safe, short passes. Eventually, someone on the Bucs would make an error or miss a tackle, and a small play would turn into a big one.

Through the first three quarters, the best Kurt could do was get the Rams a field goal. The defense added two more points with a safety, but the Bucs kicked a pair of field goals to grab a 6–5 lead. Kurt waited patiently for an opportunity, but Tampa Bay seemed like it would never make a mistake.

Finally, with less than five minutes left, Kurt took the Rams to Tampa Bay's 30-yard line. As he barked out the signals, he noticed that veteran receiver Ricky Proehl had drawn single coverage. Because he was St. Louis' slowest receiver, the Bucs were showing him little respect. Kurt knew why Proehl was on the squad. He was quick and smart and sure-handed. And this was going to be his moment to shine.

Kurt took the snap, dropped back, and made sure no one was coming over to double-team Proehl. He lofted a gentle spiral just beyond his teammate's grasp. Proehl dove for the ball, grabbed it in midair with his left hand, then cradled it against his shoulder before landing in the end zone for the winning score. The Rams were on their way to the Super Bowl!

Rams' owner Georgia Frontiere congratulates Kurt after the NFC title game.

At His Best in the Big One

chapter 7

> "He was hit and hit and hit, but he kept making plays to win the game."
>
> — JEFF FISHER, TENNESSEE TITANS' HEAD COACH

The team Kurt Warner faced in Super Bowl XXXIV could make a claim few other NFL teams could: The Tennessee Titans had beaten the Rams during the regular season. They also had pulled off one of the greatest wins in post-season history. With the final seconds ticking away in their first-round game against the Buffalo Bills, the Titans used a trick play that caught the Bills by surprise and went for a long touchdown. When Kurt saw it on TV, it reminded him of the old flag football games he played at the community center!

Prior to the Super Bowl, Kurt was surrounded by security wherever he went. As the game's biggest star, he was in constant demand.

Eddie George bulls his way into the end zone for one of his his two TDs during Super Bowl XXXIV. He and Steve McNair gave the Titans a terrific one-two punch.

There was nothing tricky about how the Titans won their other games in 1999. Quarterback Steve McNair was a good passer and a great runner. If he could not throw for a first down, he was likely to get it on foot. Tennessee's other running threat, Eddie George, was a bruising halfback who could grind out two or three tough yards or break a big run for 20 or 30. It usually took two or more tacklers to bring him down.

The Tennessee defense was spearheaded by rookie sensation Jevon Kearse. Nicknamed "The Freak" for his unusual and often terrifying combination of size and speed, Kearse had been a one-man wrecking crew for most of the season. By the Super Bowl, however, it was rumored that he was not 100 percent. This may have given some St. Louis fans a false sense of confidence, for they felt sure that Kurt and Company would roll right over the Titans.

Those fans got a rude awakening in the first half. Although the Rams were able to move the ball against the Tennessee defense, they could not put it in the end zone. Kurt got the ball into scoring position five times, but each time the Titans forced the Rams to settle for a field goal attempt. Worse, the Rams made just three of them. Luckily, the defense was playing well, so St. Louis went into the locker room at halftime with a 9–0 lead.

As the second half began, it was the Tennessee fans who began to think they had the game won.

Despite an injury, Jevon Kearse was in Kurt's face all game, forcing him to rush many of his throws.

For the game's first 30 minutes, the Titans had taken everything the Rams could throw at them and had survived. Also, right before the second quarter ended, Kurt had absorbed a huge hit and staggered off the field clutching his side. As expected, Tennessee came out strong. The Titans marched down the field into St. Louis territory, but the Rams were able to stop the drive short of the end zone. The Titans sent their field goal unit in for a 47-yard attempt. The instant the ball was snapped, Todd Lyght raced around end, launched himself through the air, and blocked Al Del Greco's kick. Eight plays later, Kurt flipped the ball to Torry Holt for the game's first touchdown and a 16–0 lead.

The Titans came right back, with Eddie George punching holes in the Rams' defense. In no time, the score was 16–6. Tennessee got the ball back and let George do his thing again. Moments later, they had another touchdown and the score was 16–13. With less than three minutes left, McNair got the Titans within field goal range, and Del Greco booted one through the uprights to tie the score at 16–16. What a game!

The whole season was coming down to one last crucial drive. Kurt had played cautiously during the second half, hoping to nurse his team's slim lead. Now he had to get

"For Kurt to step up in the Super Bowl the way he did was huge."

MARSHALL FAULK

the Rams back in gear. Kurt huddled up and barked out, "Twins Right...Ace Right...999 Halfback Balloon." This play called for him to throw to Isaac Bruce as he streaked down the right sideline. The idea was to create a footrace, which Bruce was sure to win.

Kurt took the snap and backpedaled into the pocket. As he scanned the field for Bruce, he saw something he was not expecting. "The Freak" had blasted through the blocking and was headed right at Kurt with murder in his eyes. Kurt needed to give Bruce more time to get open, but time was no longer available. Rather than scramble, he decided to release the ball early and throw it high to the spot he hoped Bruce would be. This is why teams practice the same play over and over again during a season—their timing had to be just right.

The ball left Kurt's fingertips just as Kearse buried him. It floated and fluttered down the field. Bruce glanced over his shoulder and realized what was happening. He adjusted his speed and direction to get under the ball without tipping off the man covering him that the pass was up for grabs. At the last instant Bruce made his final adjustment. He plucked the ball out of the air, let the defender's momentum take him out of the play, then zigzagged his way toward the end zone past a group of grabbing, clutching Tennessee defenders. Touchdown! "I never really got a chance to see the catch," Kurt says of the 73-yard play. "I was down on the ground. I did lift my head and saw that Isaac was running."

St. Louis fans were still celebrating when the Titans got the ball back with 22 seconds left. Their jubilation turned to terror as McNair quickly moved the ball to the St.

Kevin Dyson strains for the end zone as time runs out. Mike Jones's game-saving tackle made Kurt and the Rams Super Bowl champions.

Louis 10-yard line and then called time out. There was time for one last play. It drove Kurt crazy that his fate was out of his hands. All he could do was watch with millions of others as the Titans plotted their final try at the end zone.

McNair took the ball from center, dropped back a couple of steps, and fired a short pass to Kevin Dyson, who had veered over the middle. Dyson grabbed the ball and turned upfield—there was no one between him and the end zone! Linebacker Mike Jones grabbed his legs from behind and Dyson lunged for the goal line. Dyson crashed to the ground with his arm outstretched, straining to push the football across the goal line. When his knee hit the ground, he was just a couple of feet short.

The whistle blew. The game was over. Kurt Warner, the former shelf-stocker, was the Super Bowl MVP.

Kurt shows off the Pete Rozelle MVP Trophy and Vince Lombardi Super Bowl Trophy. His fans hope he brings home a lot more "hardware" before he is through.

What It All Means

chapter 8

"I just always felt I'd be playing football in the NFL ... or at least playing for a living."

— KURT WARNER

ootball stories do not get any better than Kurt Warner's. No one has ever come from so low and flown so high in so short a time. And no one has forced the football establishment to look at itself with such a critical eye. NFL teams spend hundreds of millions of dollars scouting, drafting, and developing quarterbacks. To do so, they have created a system for evaluating talent that ensures that they select from the cream of the crop. Imagine their embarrassment when Kurt—undrafted and invited to just one training camp in five years—became the NFL's Most Valuable Player the first time someone bothered to hand him a football.

> ## Did You Know?
> Kurt broke Joe Montana's record with 414 passing yards in Super Bowl XXXIV.

> *"On the football field I keep my emotions tied up inside. But when I'm with my family, I let them out."*
>
> **KURT WARNER**
> **WITH SON KADE**

Whether Kurt continues to put up Hall of Fame numbers, or just becomes an average quarterback, the fact remains that NFL teams need to expand their horizons. Just because a guy is not a big star in college, or just because he plays in some faraway minor league, it does not mean he lacks the skills and the heart to be a winner at the game's highest level. A few months after the Super Bowl, teams began dispatching scouts to the farthest reaches of the football world with strict orders to find the next Kurt Warner.

Kurt can only laugh when hears stories like that. When the players at Regis High were playing "Kill Kurt," could any of them have guessed that the poor 14-year-old they were after would one day shake the foundation of professional football?

Kurt tries to be philosophical about his life. He hopes to be an example for others. He tries to make sense of all the good, all the bad, and all the crazy stuff that happened in between. "I don't think I would be the person that I am had I not gone through those experiences," Kurt maintains. "As I look back, everything happened to strengthen me, to make me into this person, and develop my family the way it has become."

> "Kurt's the most grounded person you'll ever meet. Even though he's off the Richter scale right now, there's no way he'll let this go to his head."
> TODD LYGHT

Kurt cannot predict how he will fare in the coming seasons. He may remain an All-Pro, or he may not. What he does know is that he has nothing left to prove between the white lines, for he has finally found the inner peace and balance he sought for so many years. "No matter what happens on the football field," he says, "it doesn't change the kind of person I am, it doesn't change my life. I'm not going to get too overwhelmed by a situation when everything's going great, and I'm not going to get too devastated when things go bad."

Some people spend their entire NFL careers searching for the answers Kurt has found. And Kurt's career is just beginning. That is why, when it comes right down to it, there may be no better player, or person, to take pro football into the 21st century.

NFL *stats*

SEASON	TEAM	ATTEMPTS	COMPLETIONS	YARDS	TOUCHDOWNS
1998	Rams	11	4	39	0
1999	Rams	499	325	4,353	41
TOTALS		**510**	**329**	**4,392**	**41**

career *highlights*

NFL Passing Percentage Leader	. . . .	1999
NFL Touchdown Leader	. . . .	1999
NFL All-Pro	. . . .	1999
NFL Player of the Year	. . . .	1999
Super Bowl XXXIV Champion	. . . .	2000
Super Bowl MVP	. . . .	2000

*Kurt gets a big kiss from Brenda after his MVP performance in Super Bowl XXXIV.
Her love and support was a big reason why he made it to the big game.*

Index